W9-CIH-383

OUT OF THIS WORLD

PLANETS

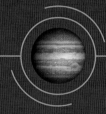

AARON DEYOE

Consulting Editor, Diane Craig, M.A./Reading Specialist

Super Sandcastle

An Imprint of Abdo Publishing
abdopublishing.com

ABDOPUBLISHING.COM

Published by Abdo Publishing, a division of ABDO, PO Box 398166, Minneapolis, Minnesota 55439. Copyright © 2016 by Abdo Consulting Group, Inc. International copyrights reserved in all countries. No part of this book may be reproduced in any form without written permission from the publisher. Super SandCastle™ is a trademark and logo of Abdo Publishing.

Printed in the United States of America, North Mankato, Minnesota
062015
092015

Editor: Liz Salzmann
Content Developer: Nancy Tuminelly
Cover and Interior Design and Production: Mighty Media, Inc.
Photo Credits: NASA, Shutterstock

Library of Congress Cataloging-in-Publication Data
DeYoe, Aaron, author.
  Planets / Aaron DeYoe ; consulting editor, Diane Craig, M.A./Reading Specialist.
      pages cm. -- (Out of this world)
  Audience: K to grade 4
  ISBN 978-1-62403-744-3
  1. Planets--Juvenile literature. 2. Solar system--Juvenile literature. I. Title.
  QB602.D49 2016
  523.4--dc23
                              2015002059

Super SandCastle™ books are created by a team of professional educators, reading specialists, and content developers around five essential components—phonemic awareness, phonics, vocabulary, text comprehension, and fluency—to assist young readers as they develop reading skills and strategies and increase their general knowledge. All books are written, reviewed, and leveled for guided reading, early reading intervention, and Accelerated Reader™ programs for use in shared, guided, and independent reading and writing activities to support a balanced approach to literacy instruction.

CONTENTS

4	Planets
5	Our Solar System
6	Mercury
8	Venus
10	Earth
12	Mars
14	Jupiter
16	Saturn
18	Uranus
20	Neptune
22	Dwarf Planets
23	Beyond!
23	Planet Quiz
24	Glossary

PLANETS

OUR SOLAR SYSTEM formed from a **swirling** cloud of dust. An exploding star created the dust. The cloud of dust turned into a star, planets, asteroids, **comets**, and other space rocks. Together they make up the solar system.

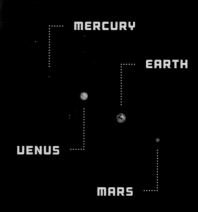
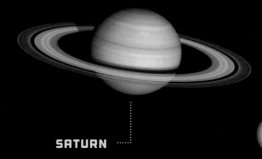

OUR SOLAR SYSTEM

MERCURY

EARTH

JUPITER

VENUS

MARS

SATURN

URANUS

NEPTUNE

There are eight planets in our solar system. Four of them are small and rocky. They are closest to the sun. The other four planets are large. They have thick, gassy atmospheres.

MERCURY

MERCURY is the closest planet to the sun. It is also the smallest planet. Some moons are larger than Mercury.

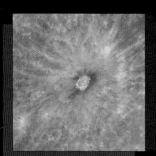

Many space rocks have crashed into Mercury. They made giant marks on the planet. The marks are called craters.

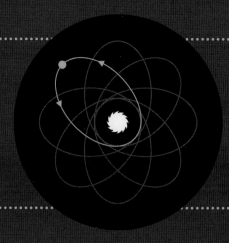

ODD ORBIT

Mercury has a strange orbit. It doesn't follow a steady path around the sun. It zigs and zags.

MESSENGER SPACECRAFT

MESSENGER started orbiting Mercury in 2011. It mapped the planet's entire surface. MESSENGER also discovered ice on Mercury's north pole.

MERCURY HAS ZERO MOONS

ONE MERCURY YEAR IS 88 EARTH DAYS

Venus

VENUS is the hottest planet.
It has a very thick atmosphere.
The atmosphere traps heat from
the sun.

OUR MOON --→

VENUS

Venus is covered with clouds. They reflect a lot
of light. This is why Venus looks bright in the sky.

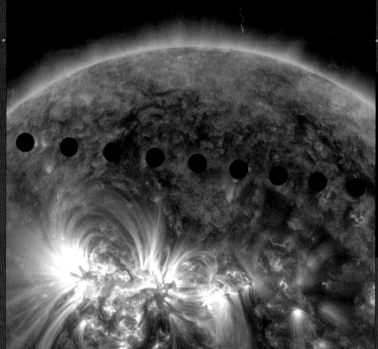

A LONG DAY!

Venus spins very slowly. One day on Venus lasts 243 Earth days. One year on Venus is 225 Earth days. One Venus day is longer than a Venus year!

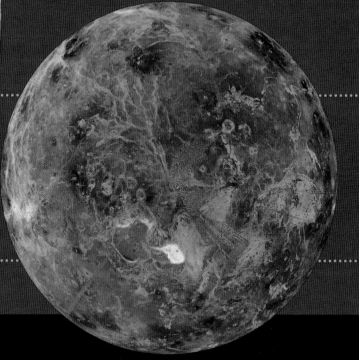

UNDER THE CLOUDS

The ground on Venus is rocky and hot. It is covered with **volcanoes**, craters, and **lava**.

**VENUS HAS
ZERO MOONS**

**ONE VENUS YEAR IS
225 EARTH DAYS**

EARTH

EARTH is the planet we live on. It is the only planet known to support life. Plants and animals need oxygen and water. Luckily, Earth has plenty of both!

Earth's atmosphere protects us from space **radiation**.

HABITABLE ZONE

Earth is in the solar system's **habitable** zone. This is the area where a planet can support life. Venus is too close to the sun. Mars is too far away from it. Earth is just the right distance.

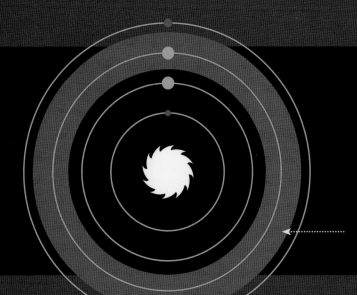

MARS
EARTH
VENUS
MERCURY

HABITABLE ZONE

THE RIGHT CLIMATE

The atmosphere works with the oceans. Together they move the air around Earth. This keeps the planet cool during the day. It keeps the planet warm at night.

**EARTH HAS
ONE MOON**

**ONE EARTH YEAR IS
365 EARTH DAYS**

MARS

MARS is a dusty and rocky planet. Scientists have studied it more than any other planet. They learned that Mars may have had oceans.

OLYMPUS MONS

MOUNT EVEREST

Mars has the largest **volcano** in the solar system. It is called Olympus Mons. It is much bigger than the largest mountain on Earth.

CALM MARS

COVERED IN DUST STORMS

DUSTY PLANET

There are strong winds around the sun. The winds blow the dust on Mars around. It goes up into the atmosphere. The dust storms can cover the whole planet for weeks!

ROBOTS ON MARS

We have sent many robots to Mars. Some of them had wheels. They explored the surface. It is **dangerous** to send a person to Mars. Robots help us safely learn about the planet.

MARS HAS TWO MOONS	ONE MARS YEAR IS 687 EARTH DAYS

JUPITER

JUPITER is the largest planet. It has a very thick atmosphere of gasses. It is called a gas giant.

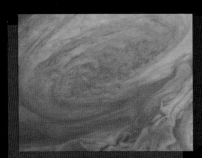

Jupiter's red spot is a **gigantic** storm. It has been there at least 350 years.

IMPACT!

Jupiter has a lot of gravity. It pulls in stray **comets** and asteroids. The **impacts** leave marks. The marks let scientists study the chemicals under Jupiter's atmosphere.

STORMY PLANET

It is always stormy all over Jupiter. There are chemicals under the atmosphere. The winds blow the chemicals around. The chemicals have different temperatures. The mixing of the chemicals creates Jupiter's colorful stripes.

JUPITER HAS
AT LEAST 67 MOONS

ONE JUPITER YEAR IS
11.86 EARTH YEARS

SATURN

SATURN is the second-largest planet. It is best known for its rings. It is a gas giant like Jupiter.

Saturn looks calm. But its atmosphere is very stormy.

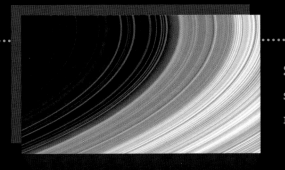

Saturn's rings are made of pieces of ice and rock. Some pieces are as small as grains of sugar. Other pieces are as big as houses. The rings reflect light from the sun. This is why they are so bright.

SATURN'S HEXAGON

There is a **hexagon** at Saturn's north pole. It is made from **swirling** gasses and clouds.

Saturn is the least **dense** planet. If Saturn could fit into a bathtub, it would float!

SATURN HAS
AT LEAST 62 MOONS

ONE SATURN YEAR IS
29.7 EARTH YEARS

URANUS

URANUS is a gas giant. But it is often called an ice giant. It has the coldest atmosphere in the solar system.

Uranus looks like a smooth blue ball. Sometimes clouds and storms create spots. This could be because of changes in the seasons.

TILTED PLANET

A planet spins on an axis. Most planets have an axis that is almost straight up and down. Uranus's axis is **tilted**. Scientists think something crashed into Uranus a long time ago. The crash is what tipped Uranus over.

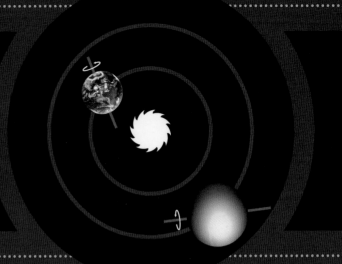

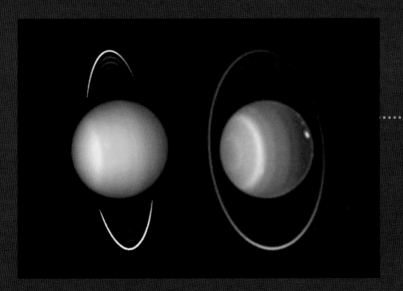

RINGS

Uranus has rings. They are made of dark space objects. They are not as easy to see as Saturn's rings. Scientists take special **photos** to see them better.

URANUS HAS AT LEAST 27 MOONS

ONE URANUS YEAR IS 84.3 EARTH YEARS

Neptune

NEPTUNE is also called an ice giant. Neptune is the farthest planet from the sun. But it is warmer than Uranus.

Neptune has the fastest winds in the solar system. The planet has a hot **core**. But its atmosphere is very cold. This causes very strong winds.

UNEVEN RINGS

Neptune is another planet with rings. They are not as even as other planet's rings. Some parts of Neptune's rings are thick. Other parts are thin.

DISCOVERED BY MATH

Neptune was discovered by math! Scientists saw something affecting the orbit of Uranus. It was like Uranus was being pulled. They did some **calculations**. The results led them to the discovery of Neptune.

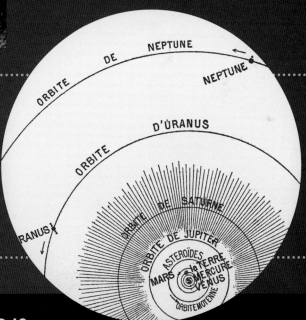

NEPTUNE HAS
AT LEAST 14 MOONS

ONE NEPTUNE YEAR IS
164.8 EARTH YEARS

DWARF PLANETS

DWARF PLANETS are larger than asteroids. But they are smaller than planets. Dwarf planets share their orbits with asteroids and space rocks. Three of the dwarf planets are Ceres, Pluto, and Eris.

CERES

Ceres orbits the sun between Mars and Jupiter. It is one of the smallest dwarf planets.

PLUTO

Pluto is an icy dwarf planet. It orbits the sun beyond Neptune. Its orbit is oddly shaped. Sometimes it is closer to the sun than Neptune. Pluto has at least five moons.

ERIS

(Artist Depiction)

Eris orbits the sun beyond Pluto. It is the largest dwarf planet we know of. It has at least one moon.

BEYOND!

Astronomers are finding planets orbiting stars other than our own. These are called exoplanets. There are more than 20 billion exoplanets in our galaxy.

PLANET QUIZ

1. What is the largest planet in the solar system?

2. Which planet(s) have no moons?

3. Mars is a dwarf planet. *True or false?*

THINK ABOUT IT!

What planet would you want to visit and why?

Answers 1. Jupiter 2. Mercury and Venus 3. False

GLOSSARY

calculation – the process or act of using math to figure something out.

comet – a mass of ice and dust that moves through the sky and develops a tail as it nears the sun.

core – the center of a space object such as a planet, moon, or star.

dangerous – able or likely to cause harm or injury.

dense – having parts packed tightly together.

gigantic – very big.

habitable – able to be lived on or in.

hexagon – a shape that has six equal sides and six equal angles.

impact – when something hits something else very hard.

lava – hot, melted rock from inside a volcano.

photo – a picture made using a camera.

radiation – energy from the sun.

swirl – to whirl or to move smoothly in circles.

tilt – to lean or tip to the side.

volcano – a mountain that has lava and ash inside of it.